CW00926010

'revised nearly every page of these volumes, besides supplying me with much of my original information, and I tremble to think how many errors they might have contained but for his generous and never-failing co-operation. Few men so excellently qualified to write a first-rate book themselves would have lent such unselfish exertion to improve the quality of another man's work."

To myself, as to almost every traveller who visited Tihrán during his long residence there, Sir A. Houtum-Schindler showed much kindness and hospitality, and it was a source of great joy to me when, on finally leaving Persia in 1911, he took up his residence at Fenstanton, only 10 miles from Cambridge, where I was able to visit him (for the state of his health did not allow him to leave his house) at frequent intervals during the final period of his life. His generosity was not confined to his knowledge, but extended even to that wherein a scholar finds it hardest to be generous, his books. In the JRAS. for 1901 (vol. xxxiii, pp 411–46 and 661–704) I published an "Account of a rare, if not unique Manuscript History of Isfahán, presented to the Royal Asiatic Society on May 19, 1827, by Sir John Malcolm". This, as I showed, was based on an Arabic original by al-Mufaddal ibn Saíd al-Mátarrúkhí, composed in 421/1030,[1] some 300 years before the Persian translation was made. On the occasion of one of my visits to Sir A. Houtum-Schindler he not only showed me another MS of the Persian translation in his possession, but also a good modern copy of the original Arabic work (hitherto, I believe, unknown) of al-Mátarrúkhí, at the sight of which I was very much delighted. A few days afterwards, on June 18, 1913, I received this precious volume from him with the following note —

[1] Throughout this article, whenever the corresponding Muhammadan and Christian dates are given together they are expressed thus, with an oblique dividing line between them, to avoid the more cumbrous "A H 421 (= A D 1030)" which I formerly employed

" Dear Professor Browne,—I beg you to accept this little book as a souvenir —Yours very sincerely, A. Houtum-Schindler."

Every scholar and lover of books will appreciate the generosity of this action, which I shall never forget.

Of himself and his life Sir A Houtum-Schindler seldom cared to speak, and the following scanty biographical particulars were all that his son, Mr L Houtum-Schindler, was able to communicate to me.

## A Short Biography of the late Sir Albert Houtum-Schindler, by his son, Mr L Houtum-Schindler

· General Sir A Houtum-Schindler was born on September 24, 1846, and in 1868 joined the Indo-European Telegraph Service in Persia, where he did excellent work under Colonel Sir John Bateman Champain, R E , and other heads of the Department He resigned in 1876 and accepted an appointment as telegraph adviser to the *Mukhbiru'd-Dawla*, then Persian Minister of Telegraphs He erected several lines for the Persian Government, and travelled through the least known parts of the Shah's Dominions to report on possible telegraph projects mines, and roads He thus acquired a wide knowledge of Persia, from its geography to its various dialects.

" In 1893 he became the first Manager of the newly-established Imperial Bank of Persia and of the Persian Mining Rights Corporation after having opened it, and after a few months became Inspector-General of the Bank, where he remained for about five years. He then entered the Persian service and became a sort of general adviser to the Persian Government, besides having charge of the Passport Office in Teheran As a linguist he excelled, and possessed a unique knowledge of Persian For his services to the Indian Government at various stages of

his life he was given the C I E in 1900, and the K C I E
in 1911, in which year he retired and took up his abode
in England.

" He was a member of the Geographical Societies of
England, Holland, Germany, and Austria, the Royal
Asiatic Society, and the Geological and Zoological Societies
of Austria, to the *Journal* of which last he contributed
a paper on the various antelopes of South Persia, including
a new species named after him, *Tragelapus Houtum-
Schindleri*  His numerous other publications are in
various languages, and include the following —

*Notes on Persian Balúchistan*, 1877
*Reisen in unbekannten Gegenden Chorasan's in 1876-77*
*Reisen im sudwestlichen Persien* (with 2 maps), 1877-8.
*Reisen im nordlichen Persien* (with 1 map), 1878.
*Reisen im sudlichen Persien* (with 1 map), 1879
*Reisen im nordwestlichen Persien* (with 3 maps), 1880-2
*Eastern Persian 'Irak* (with 1 map), 1896
*Marco Polo's Itinerary in Southern Persia*, 1881
*Marco Polo's Gamadi*, 1898
*Marco Polo's Arbre Sol, and Notes on Alamut*, 1909
*Notes on some Antiquities found near Damghan*, 1876
*Notes on Damávand*, 1888
*Notes on the Kur River in Fárs*, 1891
*Notes on the Sabæans*, 1892
*Historical Notes on South-Western Persia*, 1878
*On the New Lake between Kum and Teherán* (with map), 1888
*On the Length of the Farsakh*, 1888
*Die Parsen in Persien, ihre Sprache, u s w ,*[1] 1881
*Beitruge zum Kurd. Wortschatze*, 1882
*Weitere Beitrage zum Kurd Wortschatze*, 1886
*Neue Angaben uber die Mineralreichthumer Persiens*, 1881
*Geologie d nordwestlichen Persiens*, 1882
*Geologie d. Gegend zwischen Subzudi und Mesched*, 1886
*Eine Hebraisch-Persische Handschrift*, 1909
*Klimatafeln aus Persien*, 1909
*Coinage of the Decline of the Mongols in Persia*, 1880
*Curiosities in the Imperial Persian Treasury*, 1897
*The Shah's Second Journey to Europe in 1878*, London, 1879
*Der Semnánische Dialect*, 1877
*The Word ' Scarlet '*, 1910

[1] This is by far the best account that I know of the Zoroastrians of
Persia at the present day

' Other publications have appeared in the *Academy*
and other papers, and also various Reports, such as that
on the Turquoise Mines, besides official publications for
the Foreign Office, the Indian Government, and the
*Encyclopædia Britannica.*"

Soon after Sir A Houtum-Schindler s death I ascer-
tained that Lady Schindler was willing to sell his library,
and, eager to secure so great a treasure, I made an offer
for it which was finally accepted on January 5, 1917,
when all his Oriental MSS and such of his Persian books
as were printed or lithographed in the East passed into
my possession. The remainder of his books were bought
by Messrs W Heffer, of Cambridge. I must here express
my gratitude for the facilities granted to me by Lady
Schindler for examining and estimating the value of
these precious volumes, of which, so far as the MSS are
concerned, I now offer to students of Persian a brief
description. Of the Persian lithographed and printed
books (some seventy-five in number) I hope to give
a short description in a subsequent article

That most of the MSS. had been carefully read by their
former owner is proved by copious notes in many of
them, in some cases in the margin, but more often on loose
sheets of paper (which I have carefully preserved) lying
between the leaves    I understand that before his death
Sir A Houtum-Schindler destroyed a great many of his
papers, and all that he left in a form at all ready for
publication was a translation of the several rare works on
precious stones included in his library and described below
under the appropriate headings, besides fairly full abstracts
of the histories of Qum and Káshán, and the letters of the
great minister Rashídu'd-Dín Fazlu'lláh

Before proceeding to the detailed description of the
manuscripts, attention should be called to the peculiar
character of the collection.  In most libraries of Persian

books or MSS. it will be found that at least half the
volumes, and often a much larger proportion, are works of
poetry or *belles lettres*  In this collection there is hardly
a volume belonging to either of these classes   Historical,
biographical, and geographical works enormously pre-
ponderate, the remaining volumes represent lexicography,
anecdotes, biographies, or sayings of holy men, and various
scientific subjects, *viz*, medicine, astronomy, music, and
notably mineralogy and the natural history of precious
stones   The library is, in short, a working library,
containing many very rare books, carefully selected
during a long period of time from the point of view of
a fine scholar who was at the same time deeply interested
not only in the history, archæology, geography, and
language of Persia, but also in such practical matters as
topography, local dialects, mining, and materia medica
Personally I have never met with so comparatively small
a library (some fifty-six volumes) of manuscripts so well
chosen for a definite purpose of study, or so clearly
reflecting the outlook of him who formed it. Sir A Houtum-
Schindler s interests were essentially objective, and religious
and philosophical questions, mysticism, and *belles lettres*
did not greatly interest him   I remember once asking
him when I was in Persia whether he had paid much
attention to the doctrines of the Súfís   " No," he replied
" what is the use of trying to understand the meaning of
people who do not themselves know what they mean ? "
It must be added that a considerable number of these
MSS come from the libraries of two somewhat notable
Princes of the Royal Family, Farhád Mírzá *Mu'tamadu'd-
Dawla* and Bahman Mírzá *Bahá'u'd-Dawla*, both equally
celebrated as harsh governors and enthusiastic bibliophiles.

In the following catalogue the manuscripts are arranged,
so far as possible, according to subjects, and under each
heading in chronological order   The order of subjects is
based on that adopted by the late Dr Ch Rieu in his

British Museum Persian Catalogue, of which the older one in three volumes (1879–83) is usually cited as *B M P C*, and the Supplement (1895) as *B M P S* In the case of any book described in either of these invaluable works I have, to save space, referred, as a rule, to it only, to the exclusion of other catalogues

## CATALOGUE OF THE SCHINDLER MSS
### I RELIGION
#### (1)

روضة الأبرار (ترجمة نهج البلاغة)

The *Rauzatu'l-Abrár* ("Garden of the Righteous"), a Persian translation made by 'Alí ibn Hasan az-Zuwárí in 647/1249–50 of the celebrated Arabic work entitled *Nahju'l-Balágha*, ascribed to the Prophet's cousin and son-in-law 'Alí ibn Abí Tálib, and compiled about 400/1009–10, by Sayyid Raziyyu'd-Dín-Muhammad, a descendant in the sixth degree of the Imám Músá al-Kázim

A similar, but apparently not identical, Persian version of this work is described in *B M P C*, pp 18–19 Concerning the Arabic original, see Brockelmann's *Gesch d Arab Litt*, vol. i, p. 405.

Ff 497 of 24·2 × 16·9 c and 23 ll., the Arabic text is written in clear *naskh*, pointed, the Persian translation in *nasta'liq*, with rubrications and some marginal notes. No colophon or date of transcription. The MS belonged to Sultán Muhammad of Kashmír in 1019/1610–11, to Shamsu'd-Dawla Muníu'l-Mulk in 1198/1784, to Sir Charles Boddam in 1787, and to Kayúmairth Mírzá in 1270/1854

#### (2)

مقالات شيخ ركن الدّين علاء الدولة سمنانى

The Discourses (*Maqálát*) of Shaykh Ruknu'd-Dín 'Alá'u'd Dawla of Simnán (d 736/1335–6), beginning abruptly after a brief doxology :—

و بعده بدانکه این فواید چندست که شیخ رکن الحق و الدّین
علاء الدوله سمنانی قدّس الله سرّه میفرمود و امیر افضال
می نوشته اند و بعضی از آن اینست و السّلام علی من اتّبع الهدی

Ff 98 of 14 7 × 8 c and 14 ll , written in good *ta'líq*
with rubrications. no date or colophon. Formerly
belonged to Prince Farhád Mírzá *Mu'tamadu'd-Dawla*,
whose seal and autograph it bears, and who gave it in
Rabí ii, 1286/July–August, 1869, to one Áqá 'Abdí It is
divided into a number of sections called *majlis*

## II. GENERAL HISTORY

### (3)

روضة اولی الالباب (تاریخ بناکتی)

The well-known historical manual of Fakhru'd-Dín
Banákatí, properly entitled *Rawzatu Úlí'l Albáb* See
*B M P C*, pp 79–80, etc

This MS, which is defective both at beginning
and end, belonged formerly to Prince Bahman Mírzá
*Bahá'u'd-Dawla*, and afterwards to Prince Farhád Mírzá
*Mu'tamadu'd - Dawla* (in 1242/1826–7). It comprises
ff 185 of 23 × 15 c and 21 ll, and is written for the
most part in an ugly but fairly legible *ta'líq*

### (4)

طبقات محمود شاهیٔ گجرات

A general history from the earliest times down to
838/1434–5, defective at beginning and end, wrongly
described in a note on the fly-leaf at the beginning as the
*Ta'ríkh-i-Tabarí*, and apparently correctly in another note
as the *Tabaqát-i-Mahmúd-sháhí*, composed in Gujerat

The work concludes with sections on the biographies of famous poets, saints, ministers, and women, etc.

Ff. 550 of 27 × 17 c. and 21 ll., written in legible *taʿlíq* with rubrications; no colophon or date

(5)

مجمل فصیحی خوافی

A good modern MS of the rare *Mujmal*, or historical and biographical compendium of Fasíhí of Khwáf from the birth of the Prophet Muhammad to 845/1441-2. This manuscript, as well as another formerly belonging to Colonel Raverty, bought after his death by the Trustees of the "E. J. W. Gibb Memorial", I have described very fully, with copious extracts, in the special number of the *Muséon* (pp. 48-78) published in 1915 by some of the Belgian Professors who took refuge in Cambridge soon after the outbreak of the War, and printed at the Cambridge University Press.

Ff. 511 of 22 × 14 c. and 20 ll., written in a clear, legible modern hand with rubrications and marginal references to the context. It was copied by Áqá Bábá Sháh-mírzá'i for Prince Bahman Mírzá *Bahá'u'd-Dawla*, and completed on Muharram 17, 1273 (= September, 17, 1856)

(6)

نسخ جهان آرا

An incomplete copy (ending with the year 927/1521) of the *Nusakh-i-Jahán-árá*, a general history from the earliest times to 972 1564-5, by Ahmad ibn Muhammad al-Qádí (the Judge) al-Ghaffárí, author of the better-known *Nigáristán*, who flourished in the reign of Shah Tahmásp I, the Safawí. The contents of the book are fully stated in *B M P C*, pp. 111-16, etc

Ff. 113 of 31 8 × 19 c and 25 ll.; written in a fairly legible but ungraceful *nasta'líq* with rubrications, not dated

(7)

خالد برین

An enormous general history in five volumes entitled *Khuld-i-Barín* ("Highest Heaven"), composed in the reign of Sháh Sulaymán the Safawí in 1078 1667–8  See *B M.P S*, Nos. 34 and 35 (both incomplete), pp 22–4

The first four volumes of this MS were copied by Mullá Muhammad Mahdí Aqá Bábá Sháhmírzádí for Bahman Mírzá *Bahá'u'd-Dawla* in 1270–2 (1854–6), the last was transcribed in 1236 (1820–1). The leaves are not numbered, but the number of leaves in each volume is thus given by Sir A Houtum-Schindler in his manuscript catalogue.

*Vol. i*, comprising *Rawzas* i and ii, contains the pre-Islamic history and the history of the Prophet Muhammad and the twelve Imáms   "Ff 563 of 12½ × 8 inches and 31 lines of 6," dated Rabí' ii and Muharram, 1271 (= September, 1854 – January, 1855)

*Vol. ii*, comprising *Rawzas* iii and iv, covers the period from A H 46 to 656 (A D 666–1258), viz: that of the Caliphate and of the quasi-independent dynasties of Persia from the Ál-i-Táhir to the Sarbadárís, A H 205–747 (A D 820–1347)   Ff 285, same size as above, dated Ramazán–Shawwál, 1270 (June–July, 1854)

*Vol iii*, comprising *Rawzas* v and vi, contains the history of the Mongols from Chingíz Khán and his ancestors to the fall of their dynasty in Persia, and of Tímúr and his ancestors and descendants down to the destruction of their power in Persia by the Uzbeks Ff. 309, same size as above, dated Rajab, 1270 and 1271 (April, A D. 1854, and 1854–5)

*Vol iv* contains the history of the Safawí dynasty

down to the death of Sháh 'Abbás I ("the Great") in 1037/1627–8 Ff. 498, same size as above, dated Rabí' ii, 1272 (December, 1855).

*Vol. v* contains the remaining history of the Safawís to 1071/1660–1 It is written by a different scribe in a poor cursive *ta'líq*, and is dated Jumáda ii, 1236 (= March, 1821). Ff 173

(8)

تاریخ سلطانی

The *Tárikh-i-Sultání* ("Royal History") by Sayyid Hasan ibn Sayyid Murtazá al-Husayní, composed for Sháh Sultán Husayn the Safawí, in 1115/1703–4. It comprises three chapters, viz —

1. On Angels, Devils, and the *Jinn*, the creation of the world, and the history of the Prophets and Imáms from Adam to the Islamic period (ff. 5*b*–247*a*).

2. History of the pre-Islamic and post-Islamic kings down to the Safawí period (ff' 247*a*–290*b*)

3 History of the Safawí dynasty of Persia to the reign of Sháh Safí (ff' 290*b*–435*b*), beginning with an account of their ancestors and continuing with a detailed chronicle of events from A.H. 906–1051 (A D 1500–1641) Ff. 436 of 36 5 × 23 7 c. and 21 ll.: written in a large, clear *naskh* with rubrications Defective at end, and lacking colophon and date

(9)

زبدة التّواریخ در انساب و احوال

انبیا و اولیا و بادشاهان و سلاطین زمان از حضرت خیر البشر

آدم عمّ الی یومنا هذا،

*Zubdatu't-Tawárikh*, a general history of kings and prophets from Adam until the time of the author,

Muhammad Muhsin-i-*Mustawfí*, who was *'Ámil-i-Díwán*
in Isfahán at the time of its siege by the Afgháns in
1134/1722   The history extends to 1148/1736.  See
*B M P S*, pp 24–5, No 36, where a MS. (probably an
autograph) belonging to the British Museum (*Or. 3498*)
is fully described.

Ff 259 of 30·5 × 21 c. and 24 ll. ; written in fair *ta'líq*
with an admixture of *raqam*.

(10)

زبده التّواريخ سينندجى

A general history, sacred and profane, from the earliest
times to 1215/1800–1, compiled for Khusraw Khán,
Governor of Ardalán, in the year above-mentioned, by
Muhammad Sharíf, Qází of Ardalán, son of Mullá Mustafá
Shaykhu'l-Islám   The book comprises twelve sections
(*faṣl*), of which the last (ff 239*b*–51*b*) deals with the
reigning Qájár dynasty.

Ff 251 of 21·3 × 13·8 c and 12 ll   written in clear
*ta'líq* with rubications, and transcribed by Áqá Bábá
Shahmirzádí for Prince Bahman Mírzá *Bahá'u'd-Dawla*
It was completed on Sunday, Ramazán 27, 1275 (=
April 30, 1859)

(11)

زينة التّواريخ

A copy in two not quite uniform volumes of the
*Zínatu't-Tawárikh* ("Ornament of Histories') compiled
about 1222/1807–8 for and by order of Fath-'Alí Sháh
Qájár by Mírzá Muhammad Rizá of Shaháwar.   See
*B M.P C*, pp 135–6, and Aumer's *Munich Cat.*, p. 79.

Vol 1 comprises ff. 412 of 31·2 × 19·5 c and 29 ll, and
is written in a very neat and legible modern *naskh*.
The date 1289/1872–3 is given in a colophon on f 331 as
the date of transcription   This volume comprises the

*Agház* (Introduction) and first *Píráya*, as described by Rieu  This ends on f 311a, and after it is intercalated (ff. 333b–411b) an extract from another historical work, the *Zínatu'l-Majális* of Mírzá Rizá of Tabríz containing the history of the Safawí dynasty from the accession of Sháh Safí I (1038/1629) to its extinction, and of the Qájár dynasty down to the accession of Fath-'Alí Sháh (1211/1797)

Vol. ii comprises ff 453 (incomplete at end) of 34 × 21 5 c and 27 ll., and is written in a fair *ta'líq* with rubrications It contains the second *Píráya*, as described by Rieu (*loc. cit.*) down to 1222/1807–8.

(12)

احسن القصص و دافع النُّصَص

لاحمد بن ابى الفتح الشريف الاصفهانى

*Ahsanu'l-Qiṣaṣ wa Dáfi'u'l-ghuṣaṣ*, an abridgement of the *Ta'ríkh-i-Alfí* by Ahmad ibn Abi'l-Fath ash-Sharíf al-Isfahání, compiled in 1248/1832–3  Concerning the *Ta'ríkh-i-Alfí*, or history of 1,000 years since the *hijra*, composed for Akbar, Emperor of Dihlí, see *B.M.P.C.*, pp. 117 et seqq., Ethé's *India Office Pers Cat*, Nos 110–18 (cols 39–42), etc

Pp 534 of 28·4 × 17 c. and 19 ll., fair *ta'líq* with rubrications, last few pages much discoloured by damp, no date or colophon.  The year 994/1586 appears to be the last mentioned.

(13)

شمس التّواريخ

A general history of the Arabs, Persians, and Turks in pre-Islamic and Islamic times down to the present Qájár dynasty in Persia, entitled *Shamsu't-Tawáríkh* ("The Sun of Histories "), by 'Abdu'l-Wahháb, poetically surnamed

*Qatra*, of Chahár Mahall near Isfahán  The author,
according to a note by Sir A. H Schindler, "was a
*Mustawfi* (State Accountant) during Muhammad Sháh's
reign (A.D 1834–41)  'Alí-qulí Khán *Mukhbiru'd-Dawla*
(d. 1897) knew him "

The history comprises an Introduction, forty chapters,
and two Conclusions, the first treating of the Qájár
dynasty and the second of the Ottoman Sultáns.

Ff. 210 of 22 × 17 4 c. and 16 ll., written in fair
*nastaʿlíq* with rubrications, many marginal notes and
additions, no colophon, but has the appearance of an
autograph  A note of ownership by the author's son,
Lutfu'lláh, is dated Ramazán, 1256 (= November, 1840).

### III. HISTORY OF SPECIAL PERIODS
#### (i) *Conquest of Kirmán by the Ghuzz Turks*

(14)

عقد العلى للموقف الاعلى

*'Iqdu'l-'Ulá li'l-Mawqifi'l-a'lá*, a history of the conquest
of Kirmán by the Ghuzz chieftain Malik Dínár in 581–3
(1185–7), by Afzalu'd-Dín Ahmad b. Hámid of Kirmán.
See *B M P S*, Nos 90–1, pp. 62–3. This MS. seems to
have been copied from the same original, dated Rabíʿ i,
649 (May–June, 1251), as the two British Museum MSS
The text was lithographed at Tihrán in 1293/1876.

This MS., written in a neat and legible modern *naskh*,
was completed in Dhu'l-Qaʿda, 1269 (Aug.–Sept., 1853)
It comprises ff 77 of 15 4 × 9 6 c. and 17 ll.

#### (ii) *Muzaffarí Dynasty*

(15)

مواهب الهى (تاريخ آل مظفّر)

Two MSS. of the *Mawáhib-i-Iláhí*, a well-known
history of the Muzaffarí dynasty by Muʿínu'd-Dín of Yazd

(d 789 1387) See *B M P.C*, pp 168–9 , *B M P S*, No 50, p 33 Ethé's *Bodl Pers. Cat*, No 286 There is also a MS. in the Fitzwilliam Museum at Cambridge.

Of these two MSS the older, dated 779/1377–8, was transcribed in the author's lifetime, and was formerly in the library of Prince Farhád Mírzá *Mu'tamadu'd-Dawla* It comprises 216 ff of 21 3 × 14 5 c and 21 ll, and is written in a fine old *nasta'líq*, very legible, with rubrications.

### (16)

The second MS, undated but much more modern, formerly belonged to Prince Bahman Mírzá *Bahá'u d-Dawla*, whose seal and autograph (dated 1269/1852–3) it bears. It comprises 264 ff. of 24 4 × 13 c and 19 ll., and is written in a clear *ta'líq* with rubrications

### (iii) *Mongols and Tímúrids*

### (17)

مطلع السعدَيْن و مجمع البحرَيْن

The *Matla u's-Sa'dayn wa Majma'u'l-Bahrayn*, a well-known and valuable history covering the period from the accession of Abú Sa id the Mongol to the death of Abú Sa'íd the Tímúríd and the beginning of the reign of his successor Sultán Abu'l-Gházi Husayn, A H 727–865 (A D 1326-7—1460-1) See *B M P C*, pp 181–3, etc The author, 'Abdu'r-Razzáq ibn Isháq as-Samarqandí, was born in 816/1413-14, and died in 887 1482

The work consists of two volumes, which in this MS are bound in one volume of 441 ff of 36 8 × 28 7 c and 31 ll., vol i comprising ff 1–180 and vol ii ff 181–441 Written in legible *ta'líq* with rubrications Vol i is dated 22 Jumáda ii, 1019 (September 12, 1610). Vol. ii is undated, but a former owner's note is dated 1095/1684

(18)

طفرنامهٔ شرف الدّبن علی یزدی

The well-known history of Tímúr (Tamerlane) by
Sharafu'd-Dín 'Alí Yazdí, complete in one thick volume,
except for a page missing at the beginning and another
at the end. See *B M P C.*, pp 173–5, etc.

Ff 366 of 24 2 × 16 5 c and 21 ll.; written in an
excellent and oldish *ta'líq* with rubrications; colophon and
date missing. The beginning corresponds with the *Bibl.
Indica* ed, vol i, p 2, l 14, and the end with vol. ii,
p 743, l i

(iv) *Safawis*

(19)

سلسلة النّسب صفویّه

*Silsilatu'n-Nasab-i-Safawiyya*, a history of the Safawí
dynasty and their genealogy, by Shaykh Hasan ibn
Shaykh Abdál-i-Záhidí. The last date mentioned in the
book is Jumáda ii, 1010 ( = December, 1601). According
to a note by Sir A. H Schindler the work was composed
and this manuscript copied in the reign of Sulaymán
(A D 1077–1105 = A D. 1667–1694)

Ff. 88 of 26 3 × 16 5 c and 15 ll , written in fair *ta'líq*
with rubrications ; no date or colophon.

(20)

تأريخ عالم آرای عبّاسی تألیف اسکندر منشی

Two volumes, not uniform, of the *Ta'ríkh-i-'Alam-árá-
yi 'Abbásí* of Iskandar Munshí, a history of the life and
reign of Sháh 'Abbás I and his predecessors, composed in
1025/1616. See *B M P C*, pp 185–8, etc

Vol i, which contains twelve preliminary *Maqálát*, or
Discourses, and the first *Sahífa*, extending to the date of

Sháh 'Abbás's coronation, was copied in 1095/1684, and was formerly in the library of Muhammad Hasan Khán *Sani'u'd-Daula*. It comprises ff 279 of 27·2 × 16 5 c and 19 ll., and is written in a small, neat *ta'líq*.

Vol. ii, much larger in size, contains the reign of Sháh 'Abbás the Great (996–1038 = 1588–1628) down to his death    This volume comprises ff. 338 of 32 × 19 c and 23 ll, and is written in a small, neat *ta'líq*.    The first part of this second *Sahífa* ends on f 255a, and is dated 1055/1645.    The last leaf is torn at the bottom, and the colophon and date, if they ever existed, are lost

(r) Qájárs

(21)

بَتأريخ آل قاجار

*Tárikh-i-Ál-ı-Qájár*, a history of the Qájáıs, the present dynasty in Peısıa, down to 1220/1805, by Mustafá-qulí ıbn Muhammad Hasan al-Músawí as-Saıawí (of Saıáw oı Saráb) as-Sabalání, who wrote it ın 1269/1852–3, at the request of Qahramán Mıızá, Governor of Ázaıbáyján.

Ff 74 of 22 7 × 13·8 c. and 13 ll., good, clear *ta'líq* with gold-ruled maıgıns    Dated Muharram, 1274 (= August–September, 1857)

(22)

تأريخ ذو القرنَيْن

*Tárikh-i-Dhu'l-Qarnayn*, a history of Fath-Alí Sháh Qájár, by Mıızá Fazlu'lláh, poetically surnamed *Kháwarí*    It is dıvıded ınto two volumes and a Conclusion (*Khátıma*)

Vol i, concluded on the 6th of Rabí' ii, 1249 (= August 23, 1833), contains the fiıst thirty yeaıs of the reign (A.H. 1212–41 = A D 1798–1826), and occupies ff. 2b–185a.    The tıanscıiption of this was completed on the 10th of Sha'bán, 1257 (= Septembeı 27, 1841)

Vol ii contains the remaining eight years of the reign (A H 1242-50 = A D 1826-35) and occupies ff. 185b-272b.

The Conclusion contains a list of Fath-'Alí Sháh's descendants (ff 273b-321a) Prince Farhád Mírzá, who formerly owned this MS, gave a copy of this last portion to the Hon. C A. Murray in 1855. From this the British Museum MS. **Or. 1361** (*B M.P.C*, p 201) was copied. Another complete MS, sent from Persia by Sidney Churchill, and numbered **Or. 3527**, is fully described by Rieu in his *Pers Suppl*, No 71, pp 47-8

This MS, an autograph formerly belonged to Prince Farhád Mírzá, whose seal and writing it bears It comprises ff 322 of 24 6 × 17 8 c and 25 ll, and is written in fairly legible *nim-shikasta* with rubrications. The transcription of· vol. i was completed on the 10th of Sha'bán, 1257 (= September 27, 1841)

The author was secretary, or *munshi*, to the Prime Minister (*Sadr-i-A'zam*) Muhammad Shafí'

(23)

تأريخ ميرزا مسعود و غيره

A volume of ff 176 of 20 4 × 16 6 c and 11 ll, undated, but written in a modern Persian *ta'líq* (except in the last part, ff 145b-73b, which is in the cipher called *raqam* and *siyáq*), and containing —

1 Curious events foretold by the stars in 582/1186-7 (ff. 9a-18a)

2 A history of the Ottoman Sultans down to the accession of Sultán Selím in 918/1512, by a certain Asadu'lláh (ff 19b-57a)

3 Curious events foretold by the stars in 1242/1826-7 (ff. 65b-6b)

4. The history of 'Abbás Mírzá *Ná'ibu's-Saltana*, by Mírzá Mas'úd, Minister for Foreign Affairs (under

Muhammad Sháh), including especially the years 1242-4
(= A D 1826-8)

5 An inventory of the movable property, especially
the books, belonging to the shrine at Ardabíl in the
year 1272/1855-6, compiled and sealed by Muhammad
Qásim-i-Safawí (fl 145*b*-73*b*).

(vi) *Indian Dynasties*

(24)

گلدسته گلشن راز در تعریف

سلطان محمّد عادل شاه،

A history of Muhammad 'Adil Sháh, entitled *Guldasta-
i-Gulshan-i-Ráz dar Ta'rif-i-Sultán Muhammad 'Ádil
Sháh*, by Abu'l-Qásim al-Husayní

Begins .—

بسم الله الرّحمن الرّحیم ، بس بود این سکّه بنام کریم ،

حمد و سپاس بی قیاس مر. ذات مستجمع جمیع صفات الخ

The author's name occurs on f 2*a*, l. 2, but the title
only in a former owner's hand on the blank page at the
beginning.

Ff 223 of 29 2 × 17 c. and 15 ll., poor but legible
Indian *ta'líq* with rubrications, defective at end and
undated.

(25)

منتخب الّلباب (جلد سوم)

Part of the third volume of the *Muntakhabu'l-Lubáb*
of Muhammad Háshim Khán, better known as Kháfí
Khán    See *B M P C*, pp 232-6, and the references
there given, especially pp. 235*b*-236*a* where a MS.
(**Add. 26265**) of this volume is described   The author
died in 1144/1731-2

Ff. 106 of 31 1 × 18 5 c and 17 ll , written in clear but
ugly Indian *ta'líq* ; no date or colophon ; ends abruptly in
the middle of a sentence

## IV  LOCAL HISTORIES
### (1) *Isfahán*
### (26)

رسالة فى محاسن اصفهان للمافروخى

A treatise in Arabic on the charms of Isfahán (*Mahasin-
i-Isfahán*) by al-Mufaddal b Sa'íd al-Máfarrúkhí,composed
in 421/1030  This is the original of the Persian History
of Isfahán fully described by me in the JRAS for 1901
(Vol. XXXIII, pp. 411–46 and 661–704), of which another
manuscript will be described immediately.

Ff. 88 of 21 8 × 14 2 c. and 18 ll. , written in a clear and
excellent modern *naskh*, fully pointed, with rubrications .
copied by Habíbu'd-Dín Abú Ya'qúb Muhammad b 'Alí
al-Asghar al-Jurbádhaqání (of Gulpáyagán), and completed
on Friday, the 5th of Rabí ii, 1277 (October–November,
1860).    From the library of Prince Bahman Mírzá
*Bahá'u'd-Dawla* (who died in the Caucasus in 1883),
from one of whose sons it was bought by Sir Albert
Houtum - Schindler   The Prince's seal and a note
(apparently in his hand) dated 1277/1860 occupy the
blank page (f 5a) preceding the text.

### (27)

تأريخ اصفهان

The Persian version by al-Husayn b  Muhammad
b Abi'r- Rizá al-Husayní al-'Alawí of the above-described
treatise of al-Máfarrúkhí on the charms of Isfahán.    Of
this Persian version I published a full account in the
JRAS for 1901 (Vol XXXIII, pp 411–46 and 661–704),
based on the Royal Asiatic Society's MS (No 180), with

a note on the Schefer MS (Bibliothèque Nationale, Paris, **Suppl. persan, 1573**)

Ff 108 of 22 × 14·8 c. and 15 ll, written in good *ta'líq*, with rubrications, between red and gold borders No date or colophon. Formerly in the library of *Ihtishámu'd-Dawla*

(28)

نصف جهان فى تأريخ اصفهان

An account of Isfahán, partly topographical, partly historical, entitled *Nisf-i-Jahán fí ta'ríkh-i-Isfahán*, composed by Muhammad Mahdí b Muhammad Rizá of Isfahán in 1303/1885–6, and transcribed in Rajab, 1308 (February–March, 1891)

The historical portion of this work begins with section v on f 90a. There is a fairly detailed account of the Afghán invasion and the overthrow of the Safawí dynasty beginning on f. 123a, followed by a narrative of the rise of Nádir Sháh and final extinction of the dynasty.

Ff 242 of 21·7 × 14·5 c and 18 ll Written in a very clear and good modern *naskh* with rubrications

(29)

تأريخ دار الامان قم

Part of the Persian History of Qum (*Kitáb-* or *Ta'ríkh-i-Qum* or *Qum-náma*) described by Rieu (*B M P S.,* No 88, pp 59–60) and mentioned by C. Brockelmann (*Gesch d Arab Litt*, vol 1, p 516)

The original work was written in Arabic in 378/988–9, and dedicated to the celebrated Sáhib Isma'íl ibn 'Abbád by Hasan b. Muhammad b. Hasan al-Qummí. The Persian translation was made in 806/1403–4 by Hasan b. 'Alí b Hasan b 'Abdu'l-Malik of Qum. The work should comprise 20 chapters (*Báb*) subdivided into 50 sections (*Fasl*) Of these the British Museum MS contains only

the first 5 chapters, while this MS. contains only part
(6 out of 8 sections) of the first chapter.

Ff 65 of 34 × 21 2 c and 17 ll ; large modern *nim-
shikasta* hand   The date 17 Dhu'l-Hijja, 837 (July 25,
1434) on f 65a presumably refers to the original from
which this modern copy was made

Prefixed to the above is a smaller tract (*Kitábcha-i-
tafṣíl-i-aḥwálát . . . -i-Qum*) on the same subject, written
for a certain physician named Mírzá 'Alí Akbar Khán.
It comprises ff. 36 of 22 4 × 17 c and 16 ll, and was
transcribed on Safar 6, 1305 (October 24, 1887) in a fair
modern *nim-shikasta*

(30)

تأريخ دار الامان قم

Another more complete and carefully written copy of
the Persian History of Qum, containing the first four or
five chapters out of the twenty which constitute the
whole work

Ff 115 of 28 2 × 17 c and 25 ll , written throughout in
a clear, neat, modern *naskh* with rubrications   Ends
abruptly without colophon at the account of the conquest
of Tustar (Shúshtar) by Abú Músá al-Ash'arí   It formerly
belonged to Prince *Ihtishámu'l-Mulk*, and was copied for
him when he was governor of Káshán in 1286/1869–70,
and has a few marginal corrections in his hand

(31)

تأريخ طبرستان ابن اسفندبار

*Ta'ríkh-i-Tabaristán*, a history of Tabaristán, by
Muhammad ibn Hasan ibn Isfandiyár.   Concerning this
work, of which an abridged English translation by myself,
published in 1905, constitutes the second volume of the
" E J W Gibb Memorial " Series, see the Bibliography and

list of MSS there given (p. 1), and especially Rieu's
*Pers Cat*, pp 222-3

Ff 173 of 25 × 15 5 c and 21 ll ; written in fair *ta'líq*
with rubrications, and dated Jumáda i, 1268 ( = February-
March, 1852)  From the library of Prince Farhád Mirzá
*Mu'tamadu d-Dawla*, in whose handwriting are some
notes on Herát on the last blank page at the end   On
the fly-leaf at the beginning are some quatrains in the
Mázandarání dialect in the handwriting of Rizá-qulí Khán
*Lálá-báshí*, poetically surnamed *Hidáyat*.

(32)

تأريخ مازندران ظهيرالدّين

*Ta'ríkh-i-Mázandarán*, a history of the province of
Mázandarán by Ẓahíru'd-Dín ibn Sayyid Naṣíru'd-Dín-i-
Mar'ashí, composed in 881/1476-7   The text was edited
by Dorn (St Petersburg, 1850)  See Rieu's *B M P S*,
pp. 63-4, No. 93.  The same author's *History of
Gílán*, composed in 894/1489, and described by Ethé
(*Bodleian Cat*, No 309), was published by Mr H L
Rabino at Rasht ('*Urwatu'l-Wuthqá* Press) in 1330.1912

Ff 131 of 28 5 × 18 8 c and 25 ll.. written in clear
*naskh* with rubrications, and dated Safar 14  1271
( = November 6, 1854).  Copyist, Muhammad Hasan ibn
'Abdulláh *al-Kátib*

(33)

شرف نامهٔ شرف الدّين بتلبسى

The *Sharaf-náma*, a well-known history of the Kurds
by Sharafu'd-Dín of Bitlís  The text was published by
Veliaminof and a French translation by F. B Charmoy,
both in St Petersburg, the latter in 1868-75  See
*B M.P S*, Nos 95, 96, pp. 64-5. This MS. appears to
agree with the second of these two MSS, and hence with

Veliaminof's edition. The chronicle comes down to
1005/1593-4, and this MS was copied in 1027/1618.

## V. BIOGRAPHY AND TRAVELS
### (1) *Prophets and Saints*
### (34)

ترجمهٔ سِیَر النّبی

A Persian translation by Uways ibn Fakhru'd-Dín ibn
Hasan ibn Isma'íl al-Mú'minábádí of the Arabic biography
of the Prophet Muhammad (*Siyaru'n-Nabí*) of Sa'íd ibn
Mas'úd ibn Muhammad ibn Mas'úd of Kázarún, who died
in 758/1357. The translation was completed on the 27th
of Rabí' i, 896 ( = February 7, 1491)  A colophon dated
rather less than three years later (12th of Rabí' ii, 899
= January 20, 1494) states that this manuscript (apparently the translator's autograph) was at that time in the
possession of Mawlaná Qutbu'd-Dín ibn Husayn ibn
'Umar of Táyabád, a place near Búshanj in the district of
Herát.   Concerning Mú'minábád, the author's native
place, Sir A. H Schindler has the following note:
" Mú'minábád, a district in the Qáyin province, Khurásán,
with ruins of the old castle Mú'minábád of the Assassins."

The book is divided into four *Qisms*, each of which is
divided into numerous chapters (*Báb*), which are further
subdivided into sections (*Fasl*)

Ff 275 of 24 8 × 17·5 c. and 20 ll ; written in a large
clear *naskh* with rubrications.

### (35)

نفحات الانس

An excellent and ancient copy of Jámí's well-known
biographies of Súfi saints entitled *Nafahátu l-Uns*. This
work was composed, as stated in a chronogram at the end,
in 883/1478-9, and this manuscript was transcribed less

than twenty years later, in Rajab, 902 (= March, 1497)
It was formerly in the library of Prince Farhád Mírzá
*Mu'tamadu'd-Daula*   The text was published by
W. Nassau Lees in 1859 at Calcutta   See Rieu's *Persian
Catalogue*, pp 349–51, etc.

Ff 312 of 24 4 × 16·3 c. and 21 ll. ; good clear *naskh*
with rubrications

### (11) *Poets*

### (36)

تذكرة الشعراء دولتشاه

The well-known "Memoirs of the Poets" (*Tadhkiratu
'sh-Shu'ará*) of Dawlatsháh of Samarqand. See the Preface
to my edition of the text, published by Brill of Leyden
and Luzac of London in 1901, which contains an account
of the author and his work, and an enumeration of the
principal manuscripts

Ff. 185 of 22 3 × 16 c. and 21 ll., clear *nasta'líq*,
transcribed in "٩٨", presumably 908/1502–3 or 980/
1572–3

### (37)

تذكرة دلكشا

*Tadhkira-i-Dil-gushá*, biographies of modern Persian
poets, with extracts from their works to which is prefixed
an account of Shíráz and its most notable buildings,
mosques and gardens, and somewhat lengthy notices of
Sa'di (ff. 12b–24b) and Háfiz (ff 24b–8a)  This work
was compiled by 'Alí Akbar of Shíráz, poetically surnamed
*Bismil*, by order of Husayn 'Alí Mírzá, son of Fath-'Alí
Sháh, in A.H. 1237–40 (A.D. 1822–5), and, according to
a note of Sir A H Schindler's, was much used by Sayyid
Hasan in the compilation of his *Fárs-náma*, or "Book
of Fárs".

Ff 126 of 33·5 × 21 3 c and 20 ll ; written in a clear, good, modern *naskh* with rubrications    There is no colophon, and the manuscript would seem to have been copied by or for the author.    The notices of poets occupy ff. 41a–116b and, after the mention of Fath-'Alí Sháh and certain other royal and noble personages, are arranged alphabetically according to the final letter of the *takhallus* or *nom de guerre* (ff 48a–116b)    The author concludes the work with a notice of himself

(iii) *Travel*

(38)

مخزن الاسفار

An account of the mission of Farrukh Khán *Amínu l-Mulk* to Europe in 1857–8, in connexion with the negotiations which followed and concluded the Anglo-Persian War, composed by Mírzá Husayn ibn 'Abdu'lláh (attached to the Mission), and entitled *Makhzanu'l-Asfár* ("The Treasury of Travels")    The book is divided into two parts, of which the first contains a narrative of the journey to Paris and London and an account of the work done, while the second part (f. 216a) contains a description of the French Departments of State and Public Institutions

Ff 275 of 21 4 × 14 c and 19 ll ; clear *naskh* with rubrications, transcribed for Prince Bahman Mírzá *Bahá'u'd-Dawla* by Mullá Muhammad Mahdí Áqá Bábá Shah-Mírzá'í, and concluded on 18 Rajab, 1276 (Feb 10, 1860)

VI. GEOGRAPHY AND COSMOGRAPHY

(39)

هفت اوليم امين احمد رازى

A fine and complete MS of the well-known *Haft Iqlím* ("Seven Climes") of Amín Ahmad-i-Rází, completed in

1002/1593–4. See *B.M.P.C.*, pp. 335 *et seqq.*; Ethé's *India Office Pers Cat.*, cols 380–499, etc.

Ff. 562 of 29 × 17 c. and 21 ll , written in good clear *ta'líq* with rubrications, copied at Ahmadábád, but undated Each *Iqlím* has an illuminated *'unwán* or title-page.

(40)

نزهة القلوب

Two manuscripts of the *Nuzhatu'l-Qulúb*, a well-known geographical work (of which the portion relating to Persia has been published by Mr G le Strange in the "E J W Gibb Memorial Series", vol xxiii), by Hamdu'lláh Mustawfí of Qazwín, who also wrote the *Ta'ríkh-i-Guzída*, or "Select History", and the very rare continuation of the *Sháh-náma* known as the *Zafar-náma* See *B M P C*, pp 418–19, for the *Nuzhatu'l-Qulúb*, and for an account of the author, pp 80–2 of the same *s v. Ta'ríkh-i-Guzída* The one known copy of his third work, the *Zafar-náma*, is described in *B M P.S*, pp 172–4

The first copy (A) comprises ff 235 of 22 8 × 17 5 c and 20 ll., small, neat *nasta'líq* with rubrications , no colophon or date , bought in Dámghán in 1876

(41)

The second copy (B) comprises ff 273 of 28 3 × 20 4 c and 19 ll., clear *ta'líq* with rubrications, dated 9th of Safar, but year omitted, copied by Suhráb ibn Hájjí Alláh Karam of Sinandaj

(42)

(١) خاتمةُ روضة الصفّا، (٢) عجايب الاشيا،

A MS of 72 ff. of 27 4 × 19 2 c. and 25 ll , written in a clear modern *naskh*, with rubrications, and containing —

1. The *Khátima*, or Conclusion (book viii) of Mir-khwánd's famous general history the *Rawzatu's-Safá*, treating of geography and biography (ff. 3*b*–44*a*)

2 The *'Ajá'ibu'l-Ashyá* (or -*u'd-Dunyá*), "Wonderful Things," or "Wonders of the World", by Abu'l-Mu'ayyad Abú Mutí' of Balkh, who wrote it, as stated in the opening lines, for the Samání ruler Abu'l-Qásim Núh ibn Mansúr (reigned in Khurásán 366-87/976–97). This must refer to a (presumably) Arabic original for on f. 46*b*, l. 9, an anecdote is related which begins, "In the year 613/1216–7, when I, this humble servant, was travelling to the Ḥijáz, I reached the shore of the Egyptian Sea." This must be presumed to be an addition by the translator into Persian

The MS is undated but modern

(43)

شهرستان و عجايب المخلوقات و غيره

A volume containing four separate treatises on geography and kindred subjects, viz —

1. *Shahristán* (ff. 1*b*–57*b*), a poem in the *mutaqárib* metre, written in Sha'bán, 977 ( =Jan. 1570), describing in some detail the cities and lands of Persia, with brief notices of other lands   The end is missing, and the author's name does not appear in the text, but is given on the blank leaf at the beginning as Ḥikmatí of Turkistán

2. *'Ajá'ibu'l-Makhlúqat* ("Wonders of Creation"), a work similar in scope to the well-known homonymous work of Qazwíní, by Muhammad ibn Mahmúd ibn Ahmad at-Tírí (? -Tabarí) as-Salmání (ff 58*a*–207*a*)

3 A treatise on astronomy and geography (ff 207*b*–40*b*), written for Ghiyáthu'd-Dín Ḥabíbu lláh, who was governor of Khurásán in 909/1503–4.

4 The *Khátima*, or concluding geographical section, of Mír khwánd's well-known general history the *Rawzatu's-Safá* (ff. 241*b*–305*b*)

The volume contains ff 305 of 34 × 23 c. and 21 ll.,
fan *ta'liq* with rubrications. The third and fourth
sections of the volume are both dated 1085/1674–5

(44)

عدد خانه‌ها و سایر بناهای دار الخلافة

باهرهٔ طهران

*A List of the houses and other buildings of the glorious
metropolis of Tihrán .. compiled in 1269/1852–3 by
command of Násiru'd-Dín Sháh Qájár.*

This valuable manuscript, probably the original copy
prepared for the late Sháh, gives a complete account of
all the houses in the Persian capital sixty-five years ago,
street by street and quarter by quarter. Except for the
explanatory title of four lines at the beginning, there is
no connected text, merely long lists of the buildings and
houses and their owners, all numbers being expressed in
the cipher called *siyáq* or *raqam*.

Ff. 188 of 21 6 × 15·1 c and from 12 to 15 double entries
(each of one or two lines), written in a moderately good
*shikasta*, no colophon or scribe's or author's name

(45)

A modern Persian Gazetteer of the World, without title,
preface or colophon, containing a list of towns and
countries in all parts of the world arranged alphabetically,
with brief accounts of each.

Ff. 166 of 33 × 21 c. and 21 ll., written in a fair modern
*ta'liq*, no date or indication of authorship.

VII  SCIENCE
(1) *Encyclopædia*
(46)

مجمل الحكمة (ترجمهٔ رسایل اخوان الصّفا)

*Mujmalu'l-Hikmat* (' Compendium of Philosophy "),

being a simplified and abridged Persian version of the
well-known *Rasá'il*, or "Tracts", of the *Ikhwánu's-Safá*,
or "Brethren of Purity" The original Arabic text of
these tracts has been published in four volumes printed
at Bombay in 1305-6/1887-9, and there is also a lithographed Persian version. Dieterici has edited, translated,
or abridged a number of them

This version appears to have been made in the time of
Tímúr The translator, whose name does not appear,
complains that previous Persian versions of these tracts,
such as the *Dánish-náma*, were either archaic, or
redundant, or enigmatical, and that therefore, by request
of the Court, he undertook this simple version, which
comprises thirty-nine tracts.

This MS. was given by the late Prince Farhád Mírzá
*Mu'tamadu'l-Dawla* to his son *Muhtashamu'l-Mulk* in
Sha'bán, 1302 (May–June, 1885). It comprises 139 ff of
14 × 8 8 c. and 17 ll., and is written in a beautiful, small
modern *naskh*. The name of the copyist and date of
transcription are not given.

(11) *Medicine*

(47)

،(١) ترجمهٔ ايضاح فى اسرار النكّاح

،(٢) رساله در اعزّ اوقات، (٣) فرّخ نامهٔ جمالى

A manuscript comprising ff. 168 of 22 × 16 8 c. and
17 ll ; written throughout in a legible *ta'líq*, and dated
on f 77*b* the 25th of Dhu'l-Qa'da, 886 (January 15, 1482).
Contains —

1. A Persian translation of a well-known Arabic work
on marriage and sexual intercourse entitled *al-Ídáh fí
Asrári'n-Nikáh* by Shaykh 'Abdu'l-Rahmán ibn Nasr ibn
'Abdu'llah of Shíráz, a physician of Aleppo, who died in
565/1169 (see Brockelmann, vol. i, p. 488, No 20)   The

Persian translation is entitled *Kanz-[or Ganj-]ul-Asrár.*
It is divided into two parts (*Juz*), of which the first
(ff 1–38a) comprises ten and the second (ff. 38a–73b)
nine chapters and a Conclusion (ff 73b–7b) The
transcription was completed on the 25th of Dhu'l-Qa da,
886 (January 15, 1482)

2 *Risála dar a'azz-i-auqát* (ff. 78b–87b), a treatise
on the most suitable times for sexual intercourse, in
seventeen chapters, without author's name

3. *Farrukh-náma-i-Jamálí* (ff 88b–168b) "A work
treating of the properties and uses of natural substances,
also of divination and astrology," by Abú Bakr al-
Mutahhar b Muhammad b Abi'l-Qásim b Abí Sa'íd
al-Jamál of Yazd *B M P C*, pp 465–6 Rieu thinks that
the correct title is *Farah-náma,* as given by Hájjí Khalífa.
The work is said to have been composed in 560, 1165

(48)

ورابادين شفائى

A work on Materia Medica entitled *Qarábádín-i-Shifá'í*,
by Muzaffar ibn Muhammad al-Husayní ash-Shifá'í See
*B M P C*, pp 473–4, where the author is said to have died
in 963, 1555–6

Ff 209 of 18 5 × 11 7 c. and 14 ll. ; written in a clear
*naskh* with rubrications, and dated in the colophon
Shawwál, 1090 (November, 1679)

(49)

مجموعهٔ رسائل طبّيّه

A collection of treatises on medicine and Materia Medica,
mostly translated from a Turkish version of the original
by Muhammad Báqir al-Músawí the physician, for Sultan
Husayn the Safawí (A D. 1694–1722)

1 The first treatise (ff 3b–47b) deals with hygiene,
especially in connexion with marriage, and professes to

be a Persian rendering of a Turkish version of a treatise composed by Nasíru'd-Dín-i-Túsí for Gházán Khán—an obvious chronological error, since the latter was born about the time (A D 1274) when the former died   The Turkish version was made by one 'Abdu'l Latíf for Sultán Ya'qúb ibn Dawlat Khán

2. A treatise on the medicinal qualities of various animals and vegetables (ff. 48b–104b), also translated from the Turkish by the above Muhammad Báqir.

3   A treatise on various wounds, injuries, and ailments, and their treatment, also by Muhammad Báqir (ff. 105a–182a)

Ff. 183 of 23 6 × 13 3 c. and 14 ll., good clear *naskh* with rubrications   The seal of a former owner is dated 1168/1754–5

(iii) *Precious Stones*

(50)

*Three Treatises on Precious Stones*

A  MS. of 118 ff. of 21 × 16 5 c  and 18–19 ll., containing —

1   The *Jawáhir-náma* (ff 1b–37b) of Amín Sadru'd-Dín Muhammad b  Mír Ghiyáthu'd-Dín Mansúr of Shíráz, composed for Abu'l-Fath Khalíl Báyandarí, copied in 1883 from a *Jung*, or volume of miscellaneous contents, in the Library at Mashhad, and copiously annotated and collated with the British Museum manuscript **Add. 23565** by Sir A. Houtum-Schindler   See *B.M P C.*, pp  464–5, and *B M P S*, No  158, pp  112–13

2   *Risála dar Ma'rifat-i-Jawáhir* (ff. 40b–94a), composed by Muhammad ibnu'l-Mubárak of Qazwín for the great Ottoman Sultán Selím I (A D 1514–20), called "the Grim" (*Yáwúz*).   Begins —

حمد پاك پا كى را سزد كه گوهر پنهان جان انسان را الخ

It is divided into an Introduction, two "Mines" (*Ma'dan*),
the first containing twenty-one "Caskets' (*Durj*) on
the precious stones, and the second eight "Treasuries"
(*Makhzan*) on the precious metals, but the text breaks off
in the middle of the sixteenth "casket" on Lapis Lazuli
(*Lájuward*).

3 *Tansúq-náma-i-Ílkhání* (ff 97*b* 118*b*), a treatise on
precious stones, etc, composed by the celebrated Nasíru'd-
Dín Túsí for Húlágú Qá'án the Mongol in Arabic, of which
this is an abridged Persian translation, comprising four
Discourses (*Maqálát*). See *B M P S*, No. 157, p 112
This copy contains only the portion dealing with precious
stones  A complete type-written translation of this work,
on which Sir Albert Houtum-Schindler had evidently
spent much labour, is one of the few finished pieces of
work left by him.

(51)

تنسوق (تنگسوف) نامهٔ ایلخانی

Another copy of the *Tansúq* (or *Tangsúq*)-*náma-
i-Ílkhání*, composed by Nasíru'd-Dín of Tús for Húlágú
the Mongol, described by Sir A H. Schindler in a pencil
note on the title-page as "very much abridged, and the
sequence of chapters different from that of the British
Museum MS. The 1st *Maqála* with four *Fasls*, and the
2nd *Maqála* up to the middle of the Pearl chapter are
missing in this"

The MS in its present acephalous state comprises
142 pp of 18 8 × 12 4 c and 13 ll, and is written in
a clear and fairly good *ta'líq*. It is dated in the colophon
the end of Jumáda ii, 973 (= January, 1566)

(52)

*Three Treatises on Precious Stones*

A MS. of 118 ff of 22 4 × 14 5 c and 18 ll containing —

1. The *Jawáhir-náma* (ff 1*b*–56*a*) of Muhammad
b. Mansúr of Shíráz, of which one copy (50, 1) has been
already described above. Dated Rabí' ii, 1259 (May, 1843).

2. *Mukhtasar dar bayán - i - shinákhtan - i - Jawáhir*
(ff 57*a*–73*b*), composed for Sháhrukh Bahádur Khán by
Zaynu'd-Dín Muhammad Jámí

3. A treatise on how to recognize the different kinds of
precious stones (ll. 74*b*–118*b*), in 42 chapters, 140 sections,
and 160 "arts" (*hunar*) This last treatise appears to
be entitled *Majmú'atu's-Sanáyi'*, or "The Compendium
of Artifices".

(53)

جواهر نامه

A third copy of the *Jawáhir-náma*, or treatise on
precious stones, of Muhammad ibn Mansúr of Shíráz,
already described (50, 1). This MS. is written in a large,
clear modern *naskh* with rubrications, and comprises ff. 84
of 20 1 × 12 5 c and 15 ll It consists of two Discourses
(*Maqála*), of which the first includes an Introduction,
twenty chapters, and a Conclusion, and the second seven
chapters and a Conclusion This treatise ends on f. 80*a*,
and is immediately followed (ff 80*b*–82*a*) by a note of the
copyist, Shafi'u'd-Dín Hasan ibn Ni'matu'lláh-i-Músawi-
i-Shúshtarí, who says that he designed it for a present
to Minúchihr Khán *Mu'tamadu'd - Dawla*, governor of
Isfahán for Muhammad Sháh Qájár. This is dated the
20th of Jumáda ii, 1260 (July 7, 1844).

(54)

(١) بهجة الرّواج (٢) رسالةٌ کرامیّةً دورة سفرچی
(٣) توزکات تیموری،

A MS of 70 ff. of 22 7 × 15 4 c and 11–12 ll, containing
1 A treatise on music, entitled *Bahjatu'r - Rawáj*

(ff 1–22), professedly translated from Arabic and Greek sources into easy Persian for Sultán Mahmud of Ghazna (reigned A D 998–1030) by 'Abdu'l-Mú'min b Safiyyu'd-Dín b. Izzu'd-Dín b. Muhiyyu'd-Dín b N'mat b Qábús b Washmgín of Gurgán, and comprising ten sections (*Fasl*)

2 Another treatise on music, entitled *Risála-i-Kirá-miyya-i-Dawra-i-Sufraji* (the two last words apparently representing the name of the author), composed for 'Alí-qulí Khán (ff 23*b*–29*a*) and transcribed in 1280/1863

3 The *Malfúzát*, *Túzukát*, or "Institutes" of Timúr (ff 31*b*–68*b*), beginning abruptly [1] —

فى تدبيرات و كنكاشها و كنكاش امور جهانگيرى الخ

Dated 1st of Safar, 1290 (March 31, 1873)

The manuscript is written throughout in a clean, modern *naskh*.

## VIII PHILOLOGY

### (55)

مجمع الفرس سرورى

The *Majma'u'l-Furs* or *Lughat-i-Surúrí*, a Persian-Persian dictionary by Muhammad Qásim b Hajji Muhammad of Káshán, poetically surnamed Surúrí, composed in 1008/1599–1600 and dedicated to Sháh 'Abbás the Great See *B M P C*, pp 498–9, etc

This MS comprises ff 258 of 29 2 × 17 c and 24 ll, and is written in a clean *naskh* hand with rubrications, and dated the 8th of Jumáda i, 1254 (July 30, 1838) The preface, in which the author enumerates the lexicographical works of which he made use, fills both sides of f. 1, and is written in a small, neat *ta'liq* It was copied from Surúrí's

---

[1] Both the beginning and end correspond to the text published at Oxford in 1783 by Major Davy and Joseph White (pp 2 and 408), but it would appear that in the MS much must be missing in the middle of the treatise.

autograph and bears a date two days later than that given above

(56)

فرهنگ رشیدی

The well-known Persian dictionary entitled *Farhang-i-Rashídí* compiled in 1064/1653–4 by 'Abdu'r-Rashíd b 'Abdu'l-Ghafúr al-Husayní al-Madaní at-Tatawí. See *B M P C.*, pp. 500–1, Ethé's *India Office Pers. Cat.*, cols 1349–51, etc.

This excellent copy, which formerly belonged to Prince Farhád Mírzá, is dated in the colophon the 6th of Dhu'l-Qaʻda, 1084 (= February 12 1674), and is written in a clear *taʻlíq* with rubrications

## IX ANECDOTES

(57)

جوامع الحكايات ولوامع الّروايات

A complete MS of the immense collection of stories and anecdotes compiled by Núru'd-Dín Muhammad 'Awfí (the author of the oldest extant Persian anthology, entitled *Lubábu'l-Albáb*) in the early part of the thirteenth century of the Christian (seventh of the Muhammadan) era under the title of *Jawámiʻu l-Hikáyát wa Lawámiʻu'r-Riwáyát*. It is divided into four sections (called *Qism*), each of which comprises twenty-five chapters, each of which in turn contains a number of stories connected with some general topic

See *B M P C*, pp 749–51, *B M P S*, Nos 391–2, pp. 245–8, Ethé's *India Office Pers Cat*, cols. 245–7, and Ross & Browne's *Cat of Two Collections of Persian and Arabic MSS* . *in the India Office Library* (1902), pp 53–4

Ff 404 of 38 × 24 5 c and 25 ll . written throughout in

a neat and legible *ta'liq* , dated the 27th of Muharram, 1059.

(58)

بستان للعارفين و گلستان للعابدين

*Bustánu'l-'Árifín wa Gulistánu'l-'Ábidín* ("The Garden of the Gnostics and Rose-garden of the Devout") (This hybrid title occurs on f 12*a*, l. 13) A collection of anecdotes of an ethical and religious character, mostly about pious and saintly personages It is divided into three chapters (*Báb*), of which the first comprises ten sections (*Fasl*), the second five, and the third two, the contents of which are stated on f 13*b* The book was compiled for the Timúríd Prince *Nusratu's-Sultana* Sultán Khalílu'lláh (807–12/1404–9) by an author whose identity I cannot discover.

Ff 114 of 24 4 × 16 8 c and 19 ll written in a legible and rather archaic *ta'liq* The colophon is dated Monday, Shawwál 23, 891 (= October 22, 1486).

## X STATE PAPERS

(59)

منسآت رشیدی

Two manuscripts in Persian and another containing an abstract in English of the letters of the celebrated minister of the Mongol rulers of Persia, Rashídu'd-Dín Fazlu'lláh (author of the *Jámi u't-Tawáríkh*, put to death by Abú Sa'íd in 718/1318)

The older MS, defective at both beginning and end, is written in a good, clear old *naskh*, and comprises fifty-three letters or despatches, dealing with political and financial matters, addressed by the minister to his sons and others who held various high administrative posts and governments in different parts of Persia and Asia

Minor. These letters, collected and edited by Rashidu'd-Din's secretary, Muhammad of Abarqúh, are of considerable interest, and calculated to throw much light on Mongol administration in Persia during the latter part of the thirteenth and earlier part of the fourteenth century This MS comprises ff 182 of 17 8 × 11 8 c and 15 ll , headings and quotations from the Qur'án, etc , in red and blue.

(60)

The second MS, which, though not dated, is quite modern, formerly belonged to Bahman Mirzá Bahá'u'd-Dawla, and comprises 138 ff of 21 6 × 16 2 c and 17 ll. The opening words correspond with f 1b, l. 1 of the older MS. The concluding words of the two MSS. also correspond, and it would appear that the second is merely a modern copy of the first.

(61)

The English summary, bound and labelled " Despatches of Rashid-ad-Din ", comprises 93 + 30 written ff of 19·1 × 15·7 c and about 18 ll. Ff 1–93 contain an abstract of all the fifty-three despatches, "copied from notes supplied by Sir A. H Schindler, and afterwards corrected by him, December, 1913 " Ff. 1*–30* contain a list of these despatches, stating to whom each was addressed, and on which leaf of the older MS it begins. This volume, as well as the older MS , was given to Mr. G. le Strange (to whom they both belong) by the late Sir A H. Schindler, in July, 1913 [1] The more modern MS. was bought by me with the remaining MSS. and books

[1] Since this was written Mr le Strange has most generously presented to me the two MSS in question

Milton Keynes UK
Ingram Content Group UK Ltd.
UKHW050611220124
436367UK00017B/234